Self-Defense for Law Enforcement Officers
Superior Impedance in Life-Threatening Situations

Auervandil

Self-Defense for Law Enforcement Officers
Superior Impedance in Life-Threatening Situations

Tâniel Abu Bergerak
Shannon Greene

Auervandil

Copyright © Auervandil Publishing. All rights reserved.
Cover Image by Martial Arts Nomad

© 2017, Auervandil Publishing

Image p. 3 by Martial Arts Nomad
Image p. 5 by Marcelo Graciolli
Image p. 15 by Valerie Everett
Image p. 25 by Linzi
Image p. 43 by Dan Nevill
Image p. 55 by Nicole Vigler
Image p. 63 by George Redgrave
Image p. 75 by Velo 4 IT
Images courtesy of Flickr Creative
Commons: pp. 5, 15, 25, 43, 55, 63, and 75
Line drawings by Shannon Greene

All rights reserved. No part of this book may be reproduced or transmitted in any form or by any means whatsoever without express written permission from the author, except in the case of brief quotations embodied in critical articles and reviews. Please refer all pertinent questions to the publisher.

All rights reserved. No part of this book may be reproduced or transmitted in any form or by any means, electronic or mechanical, including photocopying, recording, or by an information storage and retrieval system - except by a reviewer who may quote brief passages in a review to be printed in a magazine or newspaper - without permission in writing from the publisher.

ISBN: 978-1-942203-61-2

For our families first and foremost,

especially those who cannot be with us,

for friends and almost-family,

for those we train with,

for Professor Diego Bispo and his Team,

for all law enforcement officers, and

for those who keep us safe day after day,

and put themselves in danger in order to help others.

Preface

This book is for law enforcement officers in need of real-world answers to physical threats in situations that present themselves without warning. The goal is personal safety for both the officer and the suspect; and effective, fool-proof methods of re-gaining control of a dangerous situation.

There are some interesting back stories to the creation of the book. The line drawings throughout the book were originally born out of necessity rather than for the purposes of visual clarity. Those illustrations initially bridged a language barrier and subsequently became an integral part of the training process. The precision and subtlety of the self-dense movements drew from Tâniel's particular style of focusing on absolute correctness in essential details. With black belts in both judo and Brazilian jiu jitsu, Tâniel embraces an approach to self-defense that is effective and street-wise, yet true to the highest principles of the elite circles of martial arts training and competition. Speaking in his native Brazilian Portuguese, Tâniel explained that many self-defense seminars are ineffective in real life.

"You must expect a rigorous opponent," he explained calmly, "and you must take your defense to completion." A simple parry of answering one move with another move may achieve enough time to draw a weapon, or perhaps not. Tâniel immediately incorporated the notion of protecting one's firearm while at the same time understanding that in volatile situations you may not have time to draw it. Tâniel emphasized the importance that the exchange cannot end until the suspect is completely under control.

While jiu jitsu has seen a powerful resurgence in mixed martial arts contexts, it has long had the reputation of a sport for quick and complex thinkers. Its top competitors often plan five or more moves in advance, and adjust quickly as needed. For this reason, jiu jitsu is often compared to chess and many high-level competitors are chess players as well. Unlike the focus of karate, Brazilian jiu jitsu engages the opponent from standing or in ground combat, and in a skilled interplay of hand grips, leg hooks, and torso positionings that spell out sudden changes in fortune, victory snatched from the jaws of defeat, surprise, intrigue, stamina, and hidden intentions. Smaller opponents overpower larger opponents and technical skills spell likely victory against brute strength.

Speaking in simplified English and pointing to line drawings, Tâniel used his English vocabulary to maximum effect, often demonstrating his point by grabbing hold of a forearm or tricep, rather than describing a grip with words. Again and again he alluded to "detail," "pay attention," "strong," and "control," and the limited repertoire of words enhanced, rather than hindered, the drive to focus on essentials.

From the seriousness of his approach, his focus on details, and his abiding emphasis on anatomy and mechanics, Tâniel explained the essential actions, principles, and vulnerabilities of all self-defense strategies.

My role in bringing Tâniel's work to the printed page has to do with drawing Tâniel's attention to the real-world dangers that law enforcement officers face, and from an act of translation: translating his dynamic teachings into words and pictures.

Shannon K. Greene, Ph. D.
Virginia Beach, Virginia

Introduction

Police interactions involving force, particularly if a weapon is involved, have come under enormous public and institutional scrutiny. Constitutional limitations in the use of force are increasingly paired with issues of municipal and civil liability. Internet images and videos of police made by citizens and onlookers are splashed all over the web. Against this backdrop, court rulings have placed greater restrictions on police use of firearms, thus narrowing the legal protections for the use of firearms in encounters, including dangerous interactions with suspects.

The bottom line is: all law enforcement situations must aim at achieving the maximum protection of both police officers and citizens. Police officers are exposed to risk, and the officers' safety must remain a central concern at all times. "Permissible force" involves split-second judgments in situations that evolve rapidly and unexpectedly. By law and for ethical reasons, officers must only use force that is reasonable and necessary.

According to a joint publication of the Bureau of Justice Statistics and the National Institute of Justice (both are agencies within the

U. S. Department of Justice), 50% of arrests are achieved by "grabbing." (*Use of Force by Police. Overview of National and Local Data.*) Furthermore, according to that same report, only 1% of individuals who interact with police officers report that the officer used or threatened to use force. Of that 1%, 80% of force-based encounters involved grabbing, holding, and the use of handcuffs (without firearms or any weapons).

There is even evidence to suggest that in rare situations in which firearms are involved, a small proportion of officers account for a disproportionately large number of incidents involving the use of firearms. *(Use of Force by Police. Overview of National and Local Data.)* This means that statistically, the use of firearms by police officers is even rarer than the data would seem to indicate. In this context, the ability to handle rapidly evolving situations without the use of firearms is not only preferable, it is often the only legal and practical option.

The exercises in this book involve practical, hands-on solutions to the challenges of arresting an unruly or uncooperative suspect. They also explain how to handle situations that rapidly evolve into imminent danger for the arresting officer. In short, this book aims at the most effective and most practical solutions for volatile situations of all kinds.

Grabbing Your Arm with One Hand

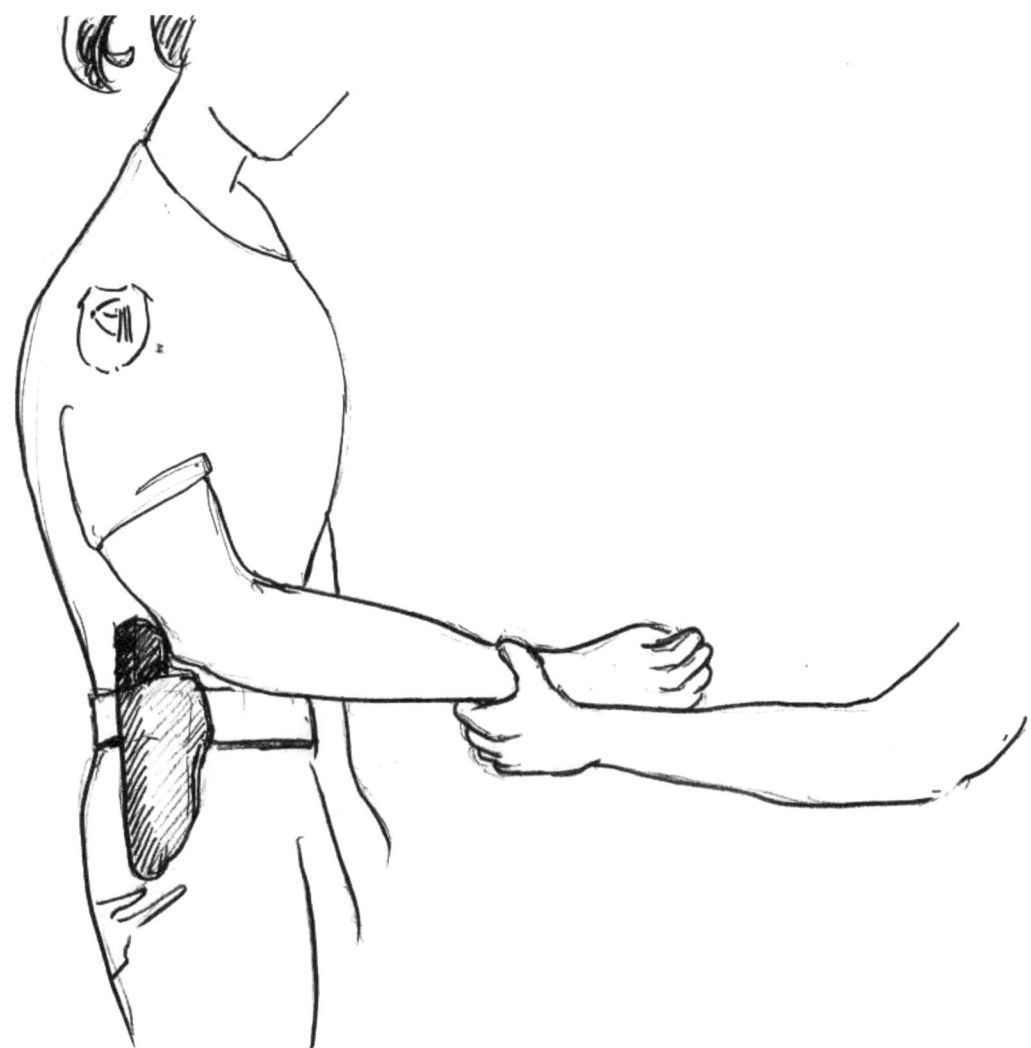

Grabbing Your Arm with One Hand

Identify the placement of the suspect's thumb. This is the weak point of the suspect's grip.

With a swift, strong movement, excecute an elbow strike into the air, pulling your wrist up and away from the suspect's grasp. This must be a strong movement, and the strength comes from leading with the elbow, not the wrist.

Grabbing Your Arm with Two Hands

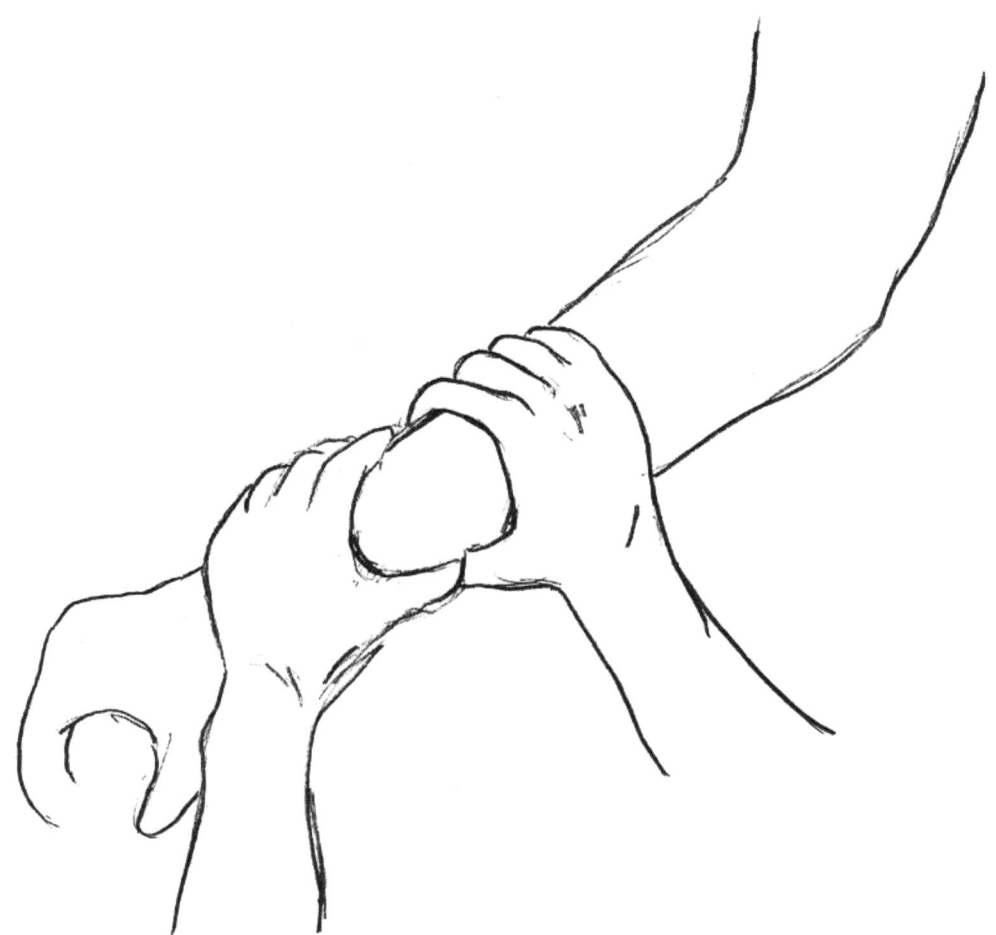

Grabbing Your Arm with Two Hands

With your other hand, clasp your own hand (the hand of your imprisoned arm), and pull your arm up and out of the suspect's grasp. Us a strong, swift motion with the strength of both of your arms.

Headlock

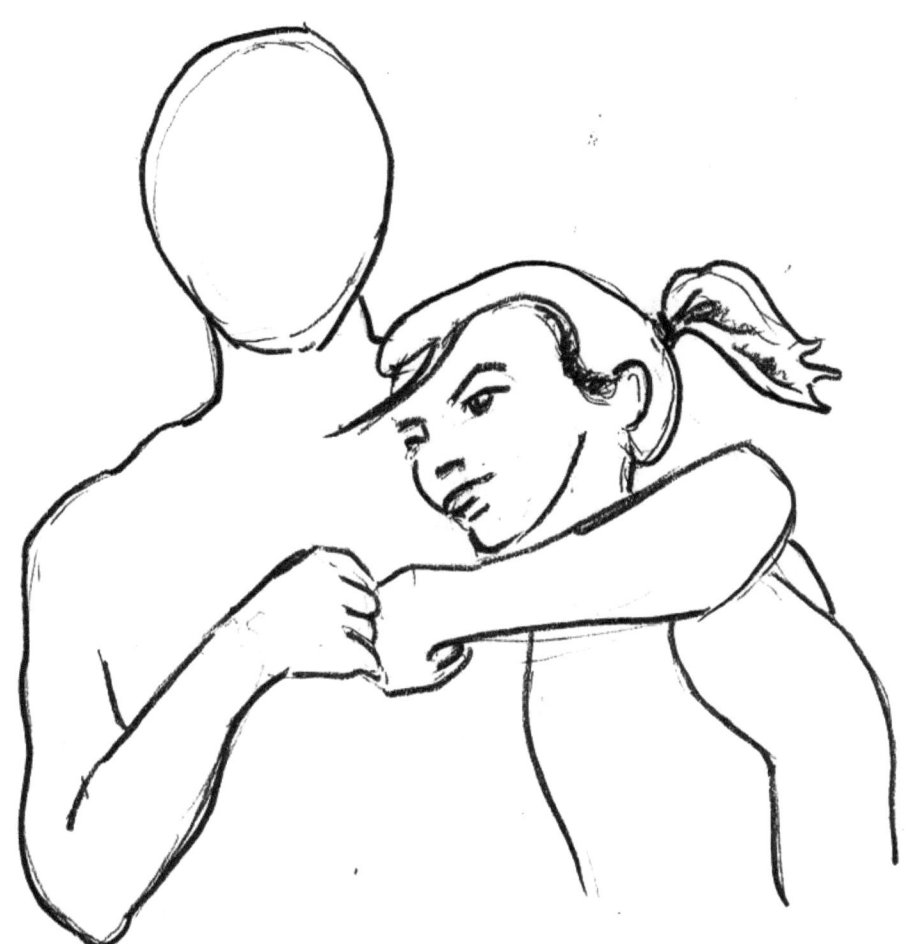

Headlock

For the style of headlock shown in the illustration, there is a simple defense.

The first priority is to defend against the suspect's other arm: the arm that is not holding you in a headlock. This is the suspect's punching arm.

With your right arm, reach behind the suspect's back and grasp his forearm near the elbow using a monkey grip (thumb and fingers on the same side).

With your left arm, grasp the wrist of his arm that is holding you in a headlock. Hold strong to that wrist.

Duck your head down and out of his headlock and pull against his wrist at the same time. Put your head down and around to his back, while using your right arm to pull his wrist to his back at the same time.

With your left hand, grasp his other wrist, bring it behind his back, and handcuff the suspect.

Headlock from Above

Headlock from Above

There is another style of headlock in which your head is held at a 90 degree angle bent forward from your body.

If you find yourself in this style of headlock, take a free arm and wrap it around his neck, placing him in a headlock. Place your other hand on the suspect's wrist. Immediately put extreme pressure on his neck and use the pressure around his neck as leverage to free yourself from your own headlock by holding his wrist and ducking down and out of his headlock.

Stabbing from Below

Stabbing from Below

Quickly cross your forearms with your right wrist over your left wrist and use the crook of your crossed arms to stop the suspect's right arm thrust.

Grasp his forearm with your right hand, controlling his arm and his knife.

Grasp the suspect's right tricep with your left hand.

Force his upper arm and forearm into a 90 degree angle as you pull his knife hand forward, down, and around to his back.

Use a wrist lock (bending his wrist toward his own forearm) to force the suspect to release his knife.

Grasping Both Sides of your Head

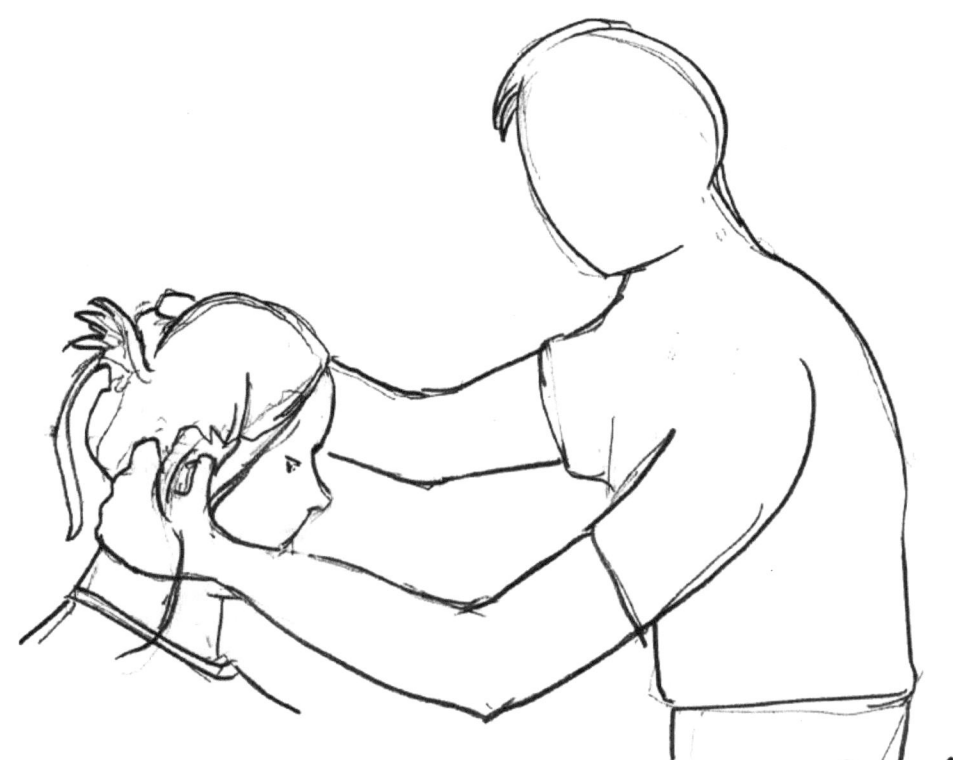

Grasping Both Sides of your Head

Hold both your arms parallel with elbows close and thread your arms upward from under the suspect's arms, in between his arms, and clasp your hands around the back of his neck.

Hold the suspect firmly and head butt your forehead to his nose. Achieve this by head butting forward at the same time as you pull his neck toward you.

Safety note: a common mistake is to attempt to use this method in choking situations. These situations involves a longer arm reach. Because of the longer arm reach, using the method described above is not possible.

Holding a Knife to Your Throat

Holding a Knife to Your Throat

There are different approaches to this situation for a citizen, but for a law enforcement officer, follow this guideline.

With at least one arm, immediately grasp his forearm with the knife in it and push the arm away. Swiftness and surprise is more important than strength.

Never assume that a knife is simply a hollow threat.

Two-Handed Choke (1st Variation)

Two-Handed Choke (1ˢᵗ Variation)

A classic two-handed choke is simple to escape.

Use both your hands to grasp each of the suspect's wrists.

Bow your head down and around in a circle at your neck, escaping his grasp.

Control his two hands at the same time as you duck down and around.

Two-Handed Choke (2nd Variation)

Two-Handed Choke (2nd Variation)

Punch your right arm straight upward into the air from below and in between both of his arms, scraping your right arm against his left arm.

Hug his neck tightly with your right arm.

Grasp his right elbow with your left hand.

Step forward with your left foot.

Use your neck hug, plus tugging his elbow, to push the suspect's body weight to his right leg.

Place your right foor behind his right calf and take him down (make him fall) using your two hand grips and a rotating motion.

Once the suspect falls, grab his wrists and bring them to behind his back for handcuffing

Drunken Suspect Coming at You with Fists Flying

Drunken Suspect Coming at You with Fists Flying

Squat low, face the suspect head on, and grasp his two thighs with your two arms.

Take the suspect safely to the ground.

Unruly Suspect Fighting from the Ground

Unruly Suspect Fighting from the Ground

In the worst case scenario, the suspect may be trained in ground tactics. In that case, avoid his legs, pass his guard to get to his side, and generally engage in classic ground combat strategies. However, for less highly trained suspects, there is a simpler solution.

With one of your arms, pull whichever of his arms is farther away from you. Pull hard until his arm is straight and you are pulling his body across the floor.

Then swiftly twist his arm, creating pressure at his elbow, and pull his arm to behind his back.

As soon as you have a suspect in a painful position, or just at the edge of pain, the suspect will likely be compliant and you can hold his arm twist as you force him into any position you wish.

Remaining calm is the best defense.

A calma é a moior defesa!

Târniel Abu Bergerak

Grabbing Your Forehead

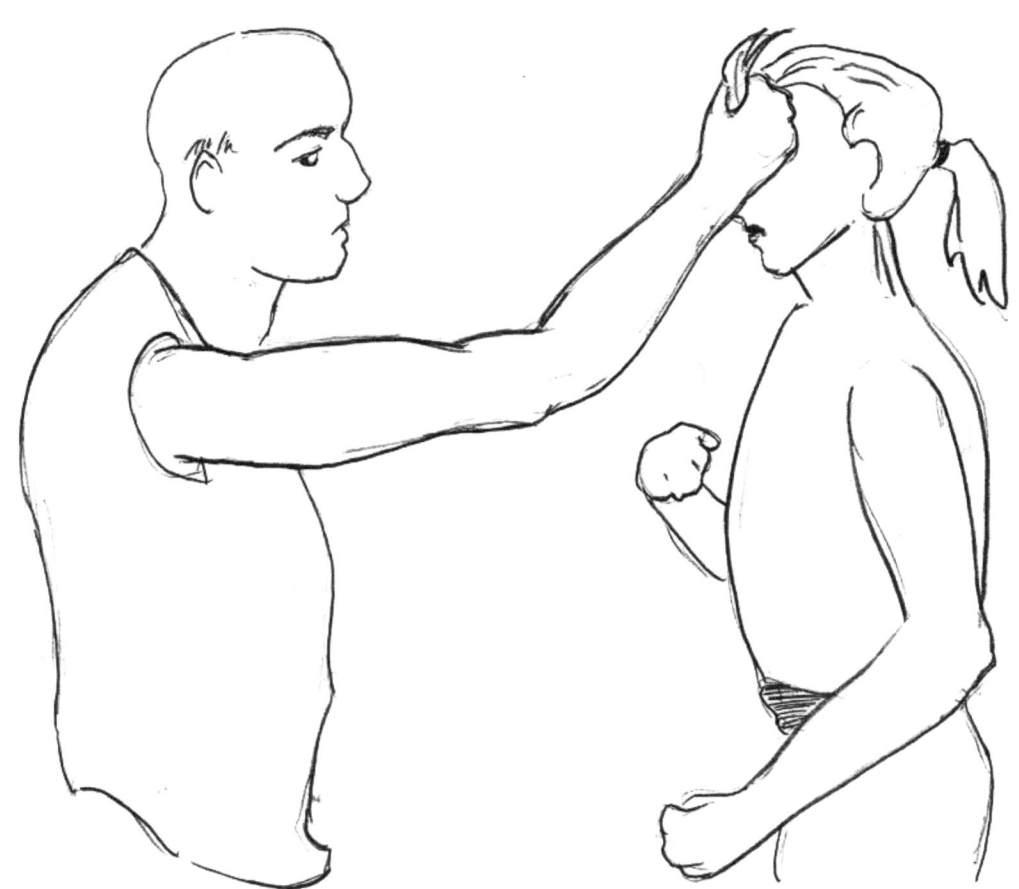

Grabbing Your Forehead

This is a dangerous position because the suspect has a free hand to throw punches.

The defense is to use your whole hand to pry his pinky finger loose, then bend his pinky back and control his arm and body from his pinky.

Bring the suspect's arms behind his back and handcuff him.

Two-Handed Waist-Level Grab from Behind (1ˢᵗ Variation)

Two-Handed Waist-Level Grab from Behind (1st Variation)

Using both hands, pry one of the suspect's pinky fingers away from his grasp. Rotate your body the short way toward the side of his body (right or left) whose arm you are controlling (but controlling his pinky).

In other words, if you pried open his left pinky, spin your body around toward his left side.

Continue walking, controlling his pinky, until you have his arm behind his back.

While still controlling his pinky, grab his other wrist and handcuff the suspect.

Two-Handed Waist-Level Grab from Behind (2nd Variation)

Two-Handed Waist-Level Grab from Behind (2nd Variation)

Squat very quickly and jump both feet down (for a squat) and at the same time about 12 inches to your right or left. Plant your feet.

Immediately reach between your feet and grab his leg with both your arms. His leg should be centered between your legs, but you will need to reach down and back with both hands in order to pull it.

Pull his leg toward you with a strong motion, causing the suspect to fall backward.

Attack by Two Suspects At Once

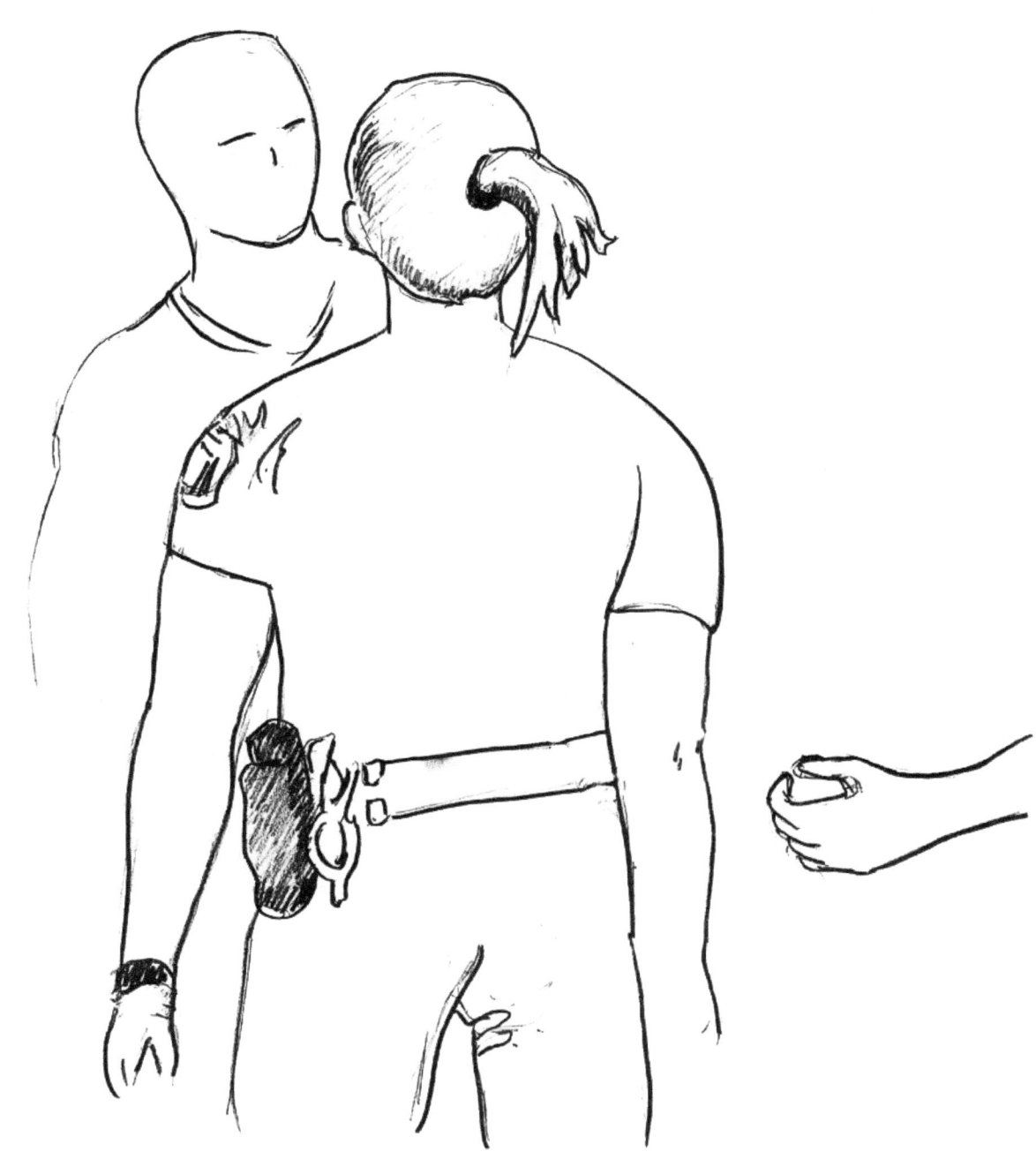

Attack by Two Suspects At Once

There is no one style of double-opponent attack, but a double attack may offer the opportunity to use one opponents body as leverage as you defend against the other opponent.

Admittedly, it is difficult to walk into the exact circumstances to set up this defense, but it is a lot of fun to execute.

If one suspect holds you at waist level from behind, lean back against him as you lift both legs and double-kick the other suspect.

After neutralizing one suspect with a double kick, squat low and to the side to break out of the other suspect's waist hold. Bend forward and reach between your legs with both arms to pull his leg toward you and up, causing the suspect to fall backward.

Two-Handed Waist-Level Grab from Behind (3rd Variation)

Two-Handed Waist-Level Grab from Behind (3rd Variation)

Swing your right leg to the left and then back behind his two legs.

Reach down and forward and grab his two thighs with your two arms, causing him to fall forward.

Arm Grab

Arm Grab

As stated earlier, a swift elbow strike into the air loosens a hand grip.

For greater control, rotate your imprisoned wrist around his wrist until he lets go, then grasp his own wrist, reversing the hold.

Stabbing from Above

Stabbing from Above

With your left arm, execute a karate-style high block to deflect and stop the advance of the suspect's right arm.

With your right arm, reach behind his right elbow from below and behind and then clasp the suspect's right wrist.

This is the wrist of the hand that is holding a knife.

With your left hand, grasp your own right wrist.

This gives you complete control of the suspect's wrist, arm, and shoulder.

By putting pressure on the suspect's shoulder, force his arm behind his back.

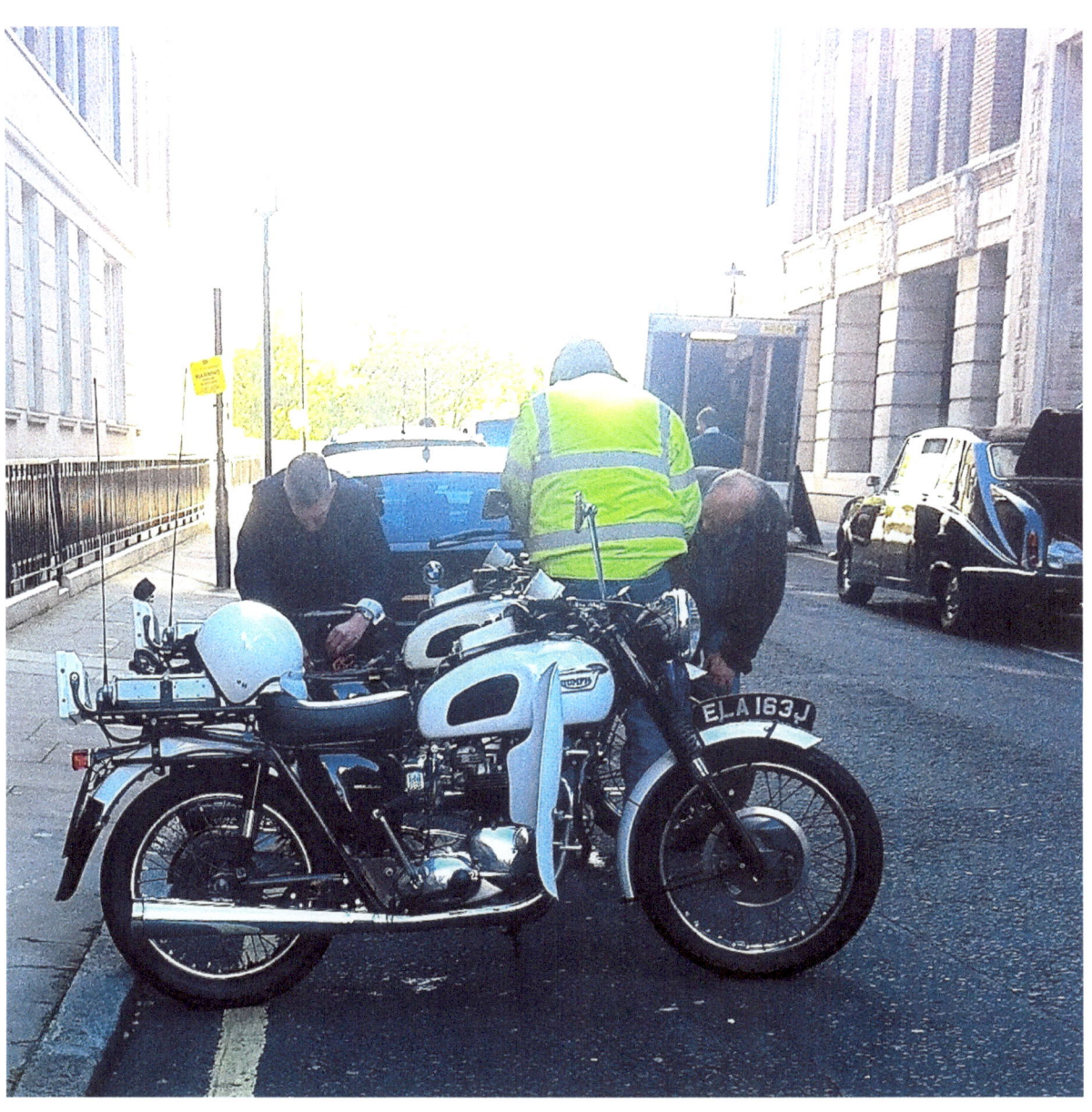

Controlling a Handcuffed Suspect

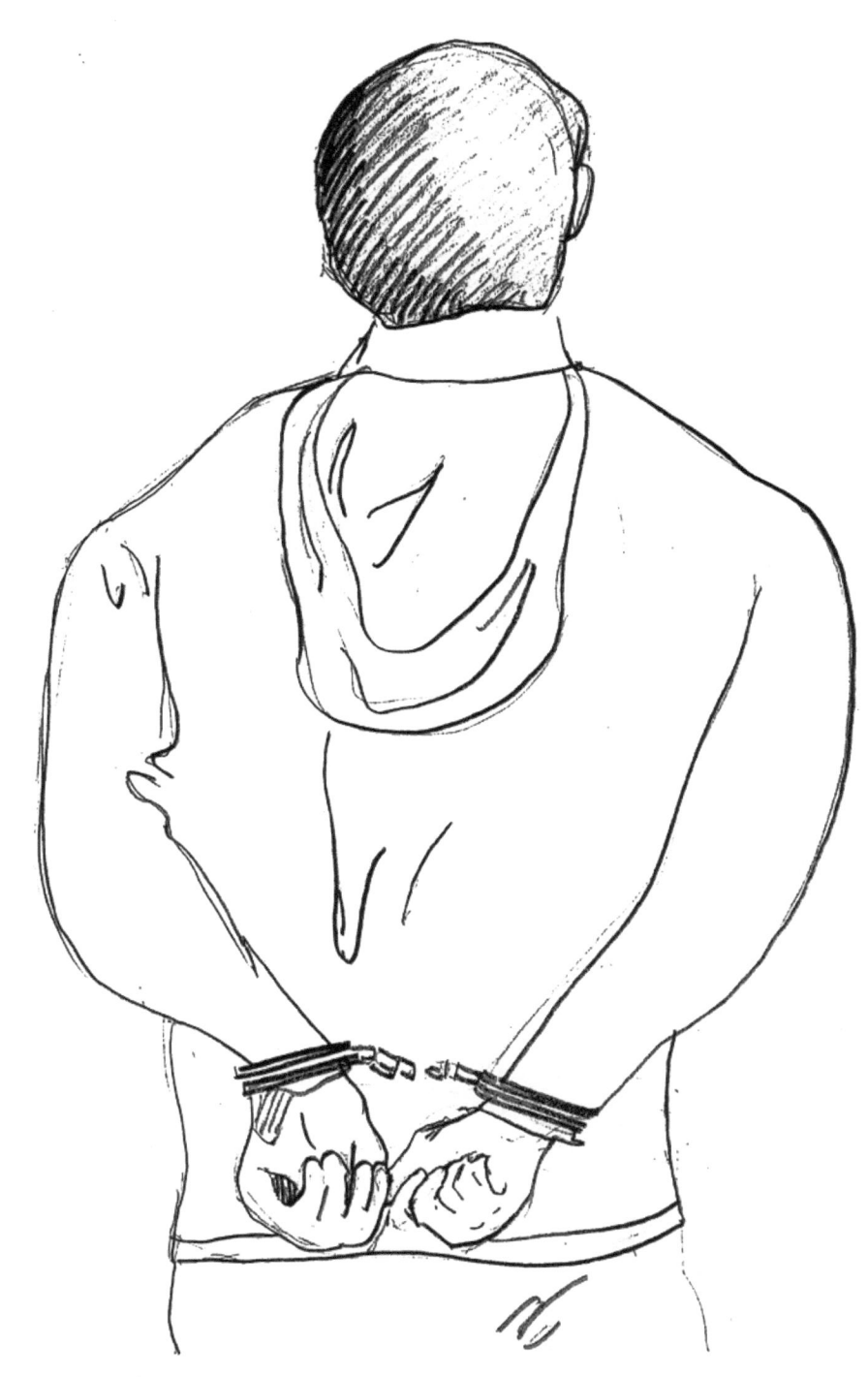

Controlling a Handcuffed Suspect

Thread your right arm from the front of the suspect's body to to his back by reaching in between his right arm and his torso. Place your right hand on his right sholder blade.

Place your left hand on top of your right hand. Using your right arm, tug down slightly with your right elbow. This will force the suspect to bend forward. Using a small amount of leverage against the suspect's right shoulder, guide the suspect to walk forward.

Grabbing Your Neck from Behind with his Forearm

Grabbing Your Neck from Behind with his Forearm

To protect your neck, try peeling a finger away or getting your left fingers between his hand and your neck. Whatever you do, control the suspect's right hand (the hand at your neck) using your left hand.

With your right hand, grab the suspect's clothing or arm at his right bicep.

Stand on your toes as you bend your knees. Drive your butt back and straight into him.

With a swift motion, straighten the back of your legs. This will lift the suspect onto your back.

Tip your right shoulder down and take him down to the ground. You can hold the suspect as he falls to control the impact.

Choking with One Hand

Choking with One Hand

Use your arm that is on the same side as the suspect's thumb.

Lift your arm with the elbow high and twist your forearm so that your palm faces away from your face.

Pry your fingers behind his four fingers and make space between his fingers and your neck.

With your other arm, grab the back of the suspect's elbow on the arm that is choking you.

With a combination of both your hands, swiftly push his elbow and pull his hand at the same time, removing the suspect's hand from your neck.

Reaching for Your Firearm

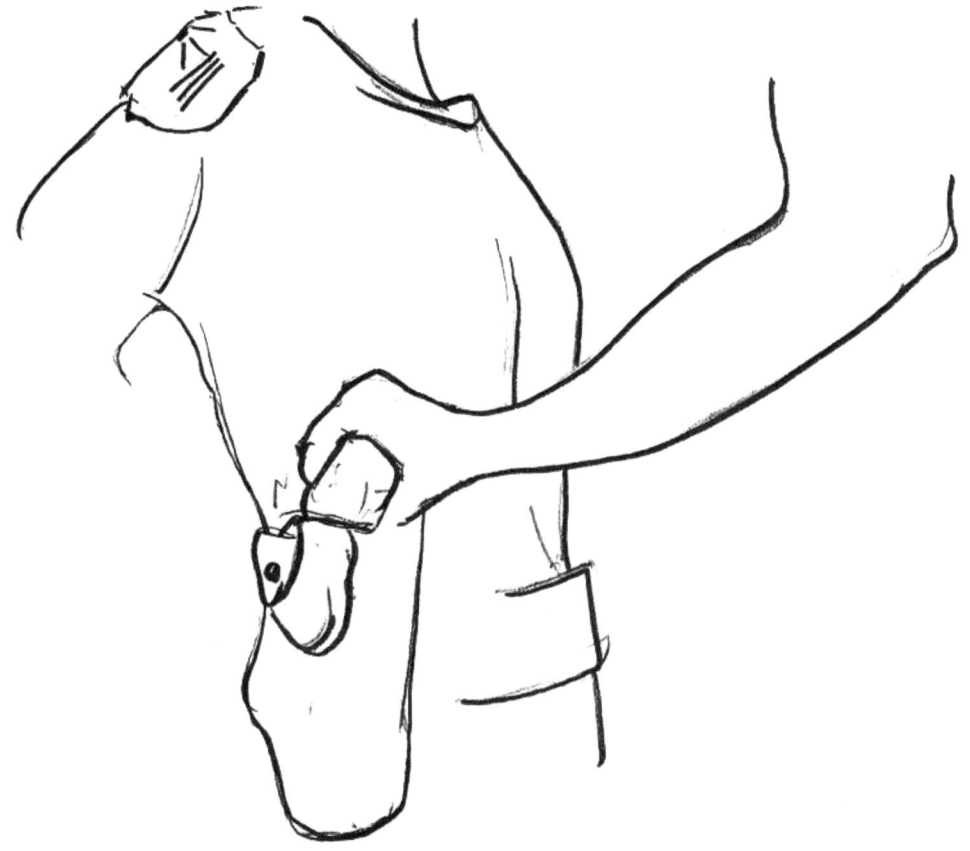

Reaching for Your Firearm

With your right hand (or whichever hand is on the same side as your firearm), grab his hand and control it by holding it down. Do not allow the suspect to remove your weapon.

Assuming you are both right-handed, the suspect's reach will be across his body.

If his hand is not holding your firearm, squeeze his wrist hard.

Place your left hand between his right arm and rib cage from his back. Push your left hand up toward the ceiling. Use both your hands to create a 90 degree angle at the suspect's elbow. Pull your left arm backward to control the suspect's shoulder.

Grabbing With One Arm

Grabbing With One Arm

With both your hands, grab the suspect's elbow, one hand from the front and one from behind.

Push the suspect's forearm toward your own body, creating pressure at his wrist.

Move the suspect's elbow up and against your body, holding the pressure at his wrist.

Epilogue

Internet images and videos tell a story, often an incorrect story, of police encounters involving force. Public uproar follows from sensationalist images, public scrutiny follows uproar, and court rulings follow, creating clarity and precise explanations of what constitutes permissible use of force. More essential than all these legal implications is the simple fact that most use of force by police officers do not involve weapons or firearms. Statistically, when the use of force occurs in police interactions, it generally involves grips, holds, and acts of restraint. In this context, martial arts training and especially grappling techniques are essential for law enforcement officers. Most importantly, officers need skills for dealing with unruly suspects and situations that escalate quickly.

Finally, the act of self-defense must never become an excuse for an unnecessary offensive strike, just as the possibility of danger should never be confused with the direct presence of danger. In dangerous situations, rely on sound yet lightning-fast reactions, good judgment under pressure, and law enforcement training, including the exercises within this book.